Esther's
Miracle at the Manger

Mitzi Probert

Copyright © 2010 by Mitzi Probert

Esther's Miracle at the Manger
by Mitzi Probert

Printed in the United States of America

ISBN 9781609575038

All rights reserved solely by the author. The author guarantees all contents are original and do not infringe upon the legal rights of any other person or work. No part of this book may be reproduced in any form without the permission of the author. The views expressed in this book are not necessarily those of the publisher.

www.xulonpress.com

ACKNOWLEDGEMENTS

Nearly 20 years have passed since the real Esther embarked on her Christmas journey. This book has represented a journey of my own. I have come to realize that it has been a journey of patience and of trusting God. It has only been through His time that this book has become a reality.

So many have been with me on my journey, encouraging me along the way. This book is dedicated to them...

To my husband Eric and sons, Kyle and Carson for their love and smiles.

To my parents, the late Bob and Retha Ring for teaching me to enjoy the simple things in life and to trust God.

To my in-laws, the late Deane and Bertha Probert who unknowingly taught me to live for the day.

To my big sister Pam and big brother Phil, for caring for their little sis and keeping the memories of life at the family farm alive.

To my late brother Gil for being an example of what true dedication and friendship means.

To the late Constance Gala, my third-grade teacher, who was the first to encourage my writing...a small class newspaper article.

To Verne Edwards, my journalism professor at OWU, for proving that red pencil marks aren't always a bad thing.

To Sharon Bozek, whose contribution of helping get the book to its final form may have been small in her eyes, means the world to me.

And finally, to my very talented illustrator Ty Schafrath, who made Esther come to life and helped make this book a reality. It has definitely been worth the wait friend.

The snow was falling lightly.
A perfect setting for the Nativity in town.

"ALL ABOARD!!" yelled Farmer Bob.
"It's time to go!"

One by one, the animals chosen for the church's Nativity walked up the ramp into the trailer.

First in were Snow and Fuzz, the wooliest sheep you ever saw. Next was Jasper the mule, Tiny the goat, and finally, **Esther** the cow.

"Oooooh, I don't know about this," Esther said to the other animals.

"Ahh, come on. It'll be fun," Tiny replied. "And this is an honor I don't want to pass up."

"Do you really think standing out in the cold in front of a bunch of strangers will be fun and much less an honor?

Noooooo. I don't think so!" said Esther.

The ride to town seemed like forever to Esther. Unlike her, the other animals were looking forward to the event.

She didn't understand what was so great about this whole Christmas thing. "Here we are. Everybody out!" Farmer Bob called. As the doors opened, the sunshine warmed the animal's faces.

They hurried to the rear of the trailer. Down the ramp Snow, Fuzz, Jasper and Tiny carefully stepped out and took their places in the Church's yard.

Esther, though, wouldn't budge. No matter how much Farmer Bob tried to coax her out, she just wouldn't move.

"C'mon girl. There's nothing to be scared about. I'm here and your friends will be with you, too."

Farmer Bob climbed into the trailer and knelt beside Esther. "Here girl. I have something for you," he said as he reached into his tattered jean jacket pocket. "I was going to give it to you for Christmas, but maybe now is as good a time as ever."

In his hand, Farmer Bob held a shiny, new brass bell.

Esther's eyes got bigger as he put it around her neck.

"How beautiful!" she thought.

"C'mon girl. Let's go show off your new necklace," Farmer Bob said while tugging on her harness.

"I know you can do this, little one. Just... take... one... step."

Suddenly, Esther's harness broke and at the same time, a car backfired nearby.

The sound spooked her so much that away she ran down the ramp, her new bell jingling in her ear.

Up the street and onto the highway she headed.

She **ran**

and **ran**

and **ran** until her legs started to *ache.*

Esther had just stopped to rest when from behind she heard a noise. When she turned around she saw bright red flashing lights coming closer. The noise kept getting louder and louder.

Ahead of her, more flashing lights, more noise. Esther was so scared. She didn't know what to do.

"I know they want to take me back to town, but I don't want to be a part of that Nativity. I have to go somewhere they'll never find me."

Esther looked around. Her only escape was to her right. To the river.

"Esther! Don't go that way!" Voices yelled all around.

But before anyone could reach her, the young cow jumped in.

The water was **ice cold** that day and moving very quickly. Esther would be lucky if she made it to the other side. "Left, right, left, right. Keep the head up. Left, right," Esther told herself. "Almost there. Only a few... more...feet to go."

Esther could barely feel her hooves as she stumbled onto the riverbank. Not even noticing the cold, Esther continued running, sliding in spots, one time even falling to her knees.

Luckily, she spotted an opening in the nearby woods, probably used by the deer.

"Maybe it will lead to some shelter or at least some food."

"I'm starving," Esther mumbled.

Indeed Esther's stomach was rumbling, enough to remind her that snow and what little grass she could find was not as tasty as the meals Farmer Bob gave her every day.

What she wouldn't give for a big bucket of that *yummy grain!*

Day soon turned to night. Too tired to walk any more, Esther laid down under a towering pine tree to sleep. It was a pleasant place, but the howling winds and rustling branches kept Esther awake most of the night.

"Ooooh, why did I run away? If I hadn't, I'd be nice and warm in the Church yard with my friends. They did have it fixed up pretty cozy," Esther said to herself.

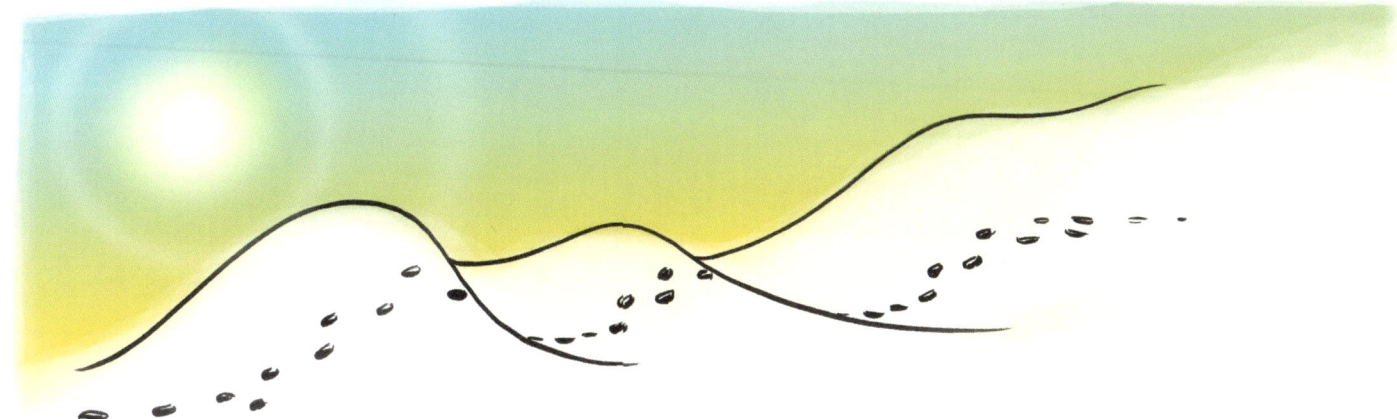

Many days passed only to find Esther still wandering through meadow after meadow and woods after woods.

"If only I could find a place to rest. Someplace like *home.*"

Just then she heard a familiar voice.

"Mooooo. Hello there, I'm Crystal. And who might you be?"

"I'm Esther."

"Esther? Are you the same Esther that ran away? I overheard Farmer Zak telling the rest of his family about you."

"Plus, I heard a bell ringing and I wondered if that might be you."

"That's me alright. Do you think I can stay here? I just can't go back there. I don't want to be there in front of all those people, especially since I don't know them.

And why do they need a cow there anyway? I'm not that important.

They have the other animals."

"Oh it's not that bad, Esther. I've done it at least five times now. As a matter of fact, I'm going to be in a Nativity in a town not too far from here tonight. It is Christmas Eve, you know!"

"Soooooo." Esther replied.

"Esther, it's a very special night and a very special honor to be chosen for a Nativity."

"***How sooooo?***" Esther replied.

"Well, at this time of year, people remember the birth of a very special baby boy, Jesus. His parents, Mary and Joseph had traveled many miles from their home to a place called Bethlehem. But because they couldn't find a room in which to stay, they ended up in a stable. It was there where a Christmas miracle happened. It was there where a king was born. A king, Esther!

And when this special baby was born many years ago, the *animals* were there to welcome him. You have been chosen to keep that tradition, Esther."

"I still don't know why they need a cow there," Esther said.

"Well, Esther, many people say that our ancestors helped keep baby Jesus from freezing in the cold night.

It was the oxen which huddled near the baby, and their breath kept Him warm."

About that time, a familiar truck pulled up by the barn.

"ESTHER!
ESTHER!

Come here ESTHER!

I've missed you!

We've all missed you!"

"That's my friend, Farmer Bob," Esther told Crystal. "Boy am I ever glad to see him! Thanks for everything, Crystal, but I think it's time for me to go. I have something *special* to do."

"You're quite welcome, Esther, and Merry Christmas!"

"Same to you, Crystal," Esther said, as she turned and ran toward Farmer Bob.

Farmer Bob gave Esther a big hug and said, "If you feel up to it, you can still come to the Church and be with your friends."

"It would be the best Christmas gift the town could receive. What do you say, Esther?"

"Moooooooo. Mooooooooooo!"

Esther replied, shaking her head so that her bell would ring.

"Well, I guess I'll take that as a yes," Farmer Bob said.

Farmer Bob opened the door to the trailer and Esther quickly ran up the ramp.

The trailer was **warm,**
 and the back of it was filled with hay.

And to top it off, Farmer Bob had placed a big **bucket of grain** there.

"**Oooooh.** I never knew I could be so cold. I guess baby Jesus must have appreciated having someone there to keep him warm,"
 Esther said to herself.

"I didn't really know we cows were that important back then, much less now. I guess I was wrong."

As Farmer Bob pulled up in front of the Church, Esther looked out the trailer window.

There were people everywhere!

Esther began to tremble, but only a little this time.

She remembered what Crystal had said, especially that she should feel proud to be a part of such a wonderful Christmas event.

The doors to the trailer opened and there stood Farmer Bob with his hand outstretched. "C'mon, Esther, they're saving a place for you...

..right next to the baby!"

ESTHER'S REAL STORY
In the early 1990s, a young cow named Esther was to appear with several other animals in a nativity scene at the First Nazarene Church in Toronto, OH. Apparently, she had other plans. Instead, Esther ran up the nearby highway, dodging traffic as she went, going several miles before jumping into the Ohio River.
Esther miraculously managed to swim across the river, then headed into the woods on the other side. She was gone for 10 days. It wasn't until Christmas eve when she was spotted on a farm near Tomlinson Run State Park in New Manchester, W.Va.

LaVergne, TN USA
26 November 2010
205976LV00002B